Playful Animals
OTTERS

Ursula Pang

PowerKiDS press

PK Beginners

Otters are mammals.

People are mammals too!

Otters have thick fur.

Otters are good swimmers.

Otters eat fish.

Otters live in groups.

Otter babies are called pups.

Otters hold hands when they sleep.

Otters love to play!

Otters play with rocks.

Otters are cute!

Published in 2025 by The Rosen Publishing Group, Inc.
2544 Clinton Street, Buffalo, NY 14224

Copyright © 2025 by The Rosen Publishing Group, Inc.

All rights reserved. No part of this book may be reproduced in any form without permission in writing from the publisher, except by a reviewer.

First Edition

Editor: Greg Roza
Book Design: Michael Flynn

Photo Credits: Cover, p. 1 Jan Peeters/Shutterstock.com; p. 3 Dan Williams Photography/Shutterstock.com; p. 5 NadyaEugene/Shutterstock.com; p. 7 Miroslav Srb/Shutterstock.com; p. 9 Kletr/Shutterstock.com; p. 11 nataliatamkovich/Shutterstock.com; p. 13 brackish_nz/Shutterstock.com; p. 15 Miroslav Hlavko/Shutterstock.com; p. 17 Erin Donalson/Shutterstock.com; p. 19 Fisher_Y/Shutterstock.com; p. 21 Susan Flashman/Shutterstock.com; p. 23 Ondrej Chvatal/Shutterstock.com.

Library of Congress Cataloging-in-Publication Data

Names: Pang, Ursula, author.
Title: Otters / Ursula Pang.
Description: [Buffalo] : PowerKids Press, [2025] | Series: Playful animals
Identifiers: LCCN 2024031108 (print) | LCCN 2024031109 (ebook) | ISBN 9781499450774 (library binding) | ISBN 9781499450767 (paperback) | ISBN 9781499450781 (ebook)
Subjects: LCSH: Otters–Juvenile literature. | Otters–Behavior–Juvenile literature.
Classification: LCC QL737.C25 P276 2025 (print) | LCC QL737.C25 (ebook) | DDC 599.769/5–dc23/eng/20240705
LC record available at https://lccn.loc.gov/2024031108
LC ebook record available at https://lccn.loc.gov/2024031109

Manufactured in the United States of America

Some of the images in this book illustrate individuals who are models. The depictions do not imply actual situations or events.

CPSIA Compliance Information: Batch #CWPK25. For further information contact Rosen Publishing at 1-800-237-9932.